Cambridge English Readers

Level 3

Series editor: Philip Prowse

Eye of the Storm

Mandy Loader

CAMBRIDGE
UNIVERSITY PRESS

University Printing House, Cambridge CB2 8BS, United Kingdom

One Liberty Plaza, 20th Floor, New York, NY 10006, USA

477 Williamstown Road, Port Melbourne, VIC 3207, Australia

4843/24, 2nd Floor, Ansari Road, Daryaganj, Delhi – 110002, India

79 Anson Road, #06–04/06, Singapore 079906

Cambridge University Press is part of the University of Cambridge.

It furthers the University's mission by disseminating knowledge in the pursuit of education, learning and research at the highest international levels of excellence.

www.cambridge.org
Information on this title: www.cambridge.org/9780521536592

© Cambridge University Press 2003

First published 2003
Reprinted 2017

Printed in the United Kingdom by Hobbs the Printers Ltd

A catalogue record for this publication is available from the British Library

ISBN 978-0-521-53659-2 Paperback

Contents

Chapter 1   Calm before the storm   6
Chapter 2   The hurricane gets closer   12
Chapter 3   The hurricane kills   19
Chapter 4   In the marina   28
Chapter 5   Good to be alive   36
Chapter 6   The *Manatee*   39
Chapter 7   The last call   44
Chapter 8   The eye of the storm   51

Characters

Ikemi: a young woman
Hiru: Ikemi's father
Max: Ikemi's boyfriend
Ross Peters: a teacher at Max's flying school
Rick and Elaine Bridges: a married couple

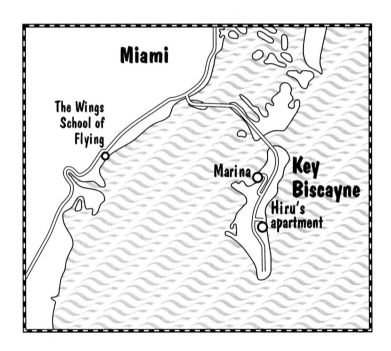

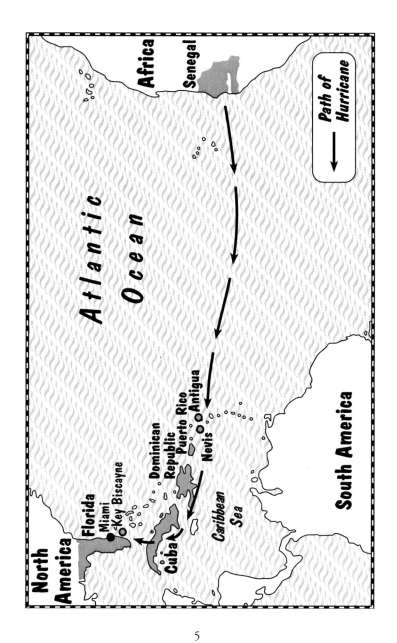

Chapter 1 *Calm before the storm*

September 9

It was a wonderful September day in Miami, Florida. On the wide white beach along the coast of Key Biscayne the sun was hot on the sand.

A slim young woman in her early twenties was lying alone down by the sea. She was beautiful, but her face was sad. Her long black hair fell over the book she was reading. From time to time she looked up from her book and along the beach. Then she put her book away in a bag and sat up. She looked unhappily along the beach again.

"I can't tell him! I just can't tell him!" she whispered to herself.

The sea was flat, calm, and clear. And the weather was hot. It was too hot to work, too hot to play, too hot to drive into Miami to meet up with friends, and it was too hot to stay at home. The wide green streets of Key Biscayne and the parking lots of the tall white buildings were almost empty in the burning sun.

Everybody was at the beach. Groups of friends lay on the sand, talking, laughing and listening to music. Some were playing ball games, others ran into the water to swim. Families with fat babies and sunburned children lay under the palm trees that grew along the beach. Mothers watched carefully as their children ran down to the sea to play in the warm shallow water. And at the far end of the beach, across the water, the tall white buildings of Miami stood out against the clear blue sky.

At the far side of the beach a narrow path ran between the tall white apartment buildings. It joined the green streets of Key Biscayne with the wide white beaches. A tall good-looking man about the same age as the woman was coming down the path. He was wearing a T-shirt and jeans and his arms and face were brown from the sun. At the end of the path he stopped under the palm trees and looked out across the beach.

"Ikemi!" he shouted.

"Max!" The woman stood up and waved. "I'm here! Over here!"

He saw her, smiled, waved back, took off his shoes, and came running towards her over the sand. He sat down beside her and moved over to kiss her.

"Max, don't."

"Don't? Don't kiss you? Why not? What's the matter?" he asked.

Ikemi looked away from Max. "I'm sorry, Max, I'm so sorry, but we have to talk. There's something I have to say to you . . . I wish I didn't . . . I really wish . . ."

"Ikemi! What's the matter? What's going on? Tell me!"

Ikemi reached down and picked up a small stone. "It's my father," she said slowly. "He doesn't want . . . you and I . . . he says we're getting too serious. He says . . ." Ikemi did not finish what she was saying. Max took hold of her shoulders and looked into her eyes.

"Ikemi! Tell me! What does your father say?"

"Oh Max! He says I have to stop seeing you. I can't see you anymore."

"Stop seeing me? But he can't do that!" Max looked at

Ikemi in surprise. But she looked at the stone, turning it over and over in her hands.

"Ikemi! Look at me! What's going on? Why does your father want you to stop seeing me? What's the matter with me? What have I done?"

Ikemi threw the stone into the beautiful clear water.

She turned and looked at Max. "It's not what you've done, Max. It's who you are."

"Who I am? What do you mean?"

"You're American, Max. I know it's difficult for you to understand, but my father does not want me to date American men. He says there are too many differences between us, between Japanese and American people, between the way we live and the way we think."

"What? You can't be serious!" said Max. "How on earth can your father say that? Your mother was American! He married her, didn't he? He married an American! How can it be all right for him to marry an American but not for you? It's crazy!"

Ikemi looked away.

"I don't know, Max, I just don't know. But I do know that he isn't going to change his mind."

Max shook his head.

"Ikemi, I don't understand. You don't agree with your father, do you? Come on! You were born in America! You've spent all your life here! You went to American schools and now you're studying at an American university! You're American too, Ikemi! You're the same as me! We're American and we're free to choose who we see and what we do! You don't always have to do what your father wants, you know."

Ikemi lifted her eyes and looked at Max.

"You're wrong, Max. I'm sorry. I'm not free. Yes, I do live here, and yes, I went to school here. But my father is Japanese and after my mother died he brought me up. I can't go against my father."

Max looked down at Ikemi's face.

"But what about me?" Max said quietly. "And what about us? Ikemi, this is crazy! Are you going to let your father decide who you should marry? Is what your father thinks more important than loving someone?"

Ikemi did not look at Max. She didn't want to see the hurt in his face.

"I'm sorry, Max, I'm really sorry," she whispered. "I . . ."

But Max stood up and walked away before she could finish her sentence.

She watched him walk slowly across the beach. She wanted to run after him, throw her arms around him, kiss him. She wanted to tell him she loved him, tell him that she loved him so much it frightened her.

At the top of the beach he stopped, turned, and looked back at her. Their eyes met for a moment and then she looked away quickly. She hated hurting him. Max was the kindest man she knew.

It did not matter to her father that Max was kind. What mattered to her father was what a man said and what he did. Her father thought the most important thing for a man was to be patient, to be quiet, to say nothing, to be brave, to be able to feel pain without talking about it. It was not surprising that he did not like Max. Max was loud, he was noisy, he did not think before he spoke, he was impatient – he was everything her father hated in a man. It did not matter to her father that Max was honest, generous and helpful. It was not important to her father that Max made Ikemi laugh and feel happy.

"Why?" she whispered to herself as she watched Max disappear. "Why do I have to choose between them?"

*   *   *

About 8000 kilometers away, off the west coast of Africa, the weather was very different from the beautiful, calm, sunny day on the beach in Florida. It was stormy in West Africa, very stormy: large waves were crashing onto the sand, and the leaves of the palm trees were blowing noisily in the wind. The beaches of Senegal were empty except for a few brave children who were jumping in and out of the waves.

The sea was empty too. All the fishermen had come back to land. They had helped each other pull their boats high up onto the beaches, away from the waves. The fishermen sat in groups, talking and laughing, happy to be on the land and not on the sea. Soon the storms would pass, the sea would become calm, and they would go out fishing again.

The fishermen were right: the storms did pass. They moved slowly west, away from the coast and out into the sea. And as they traveled over the sea, they took in the hot, wet sea air and they grew bigger and bigger. Then the storms all blew together and made one large storm. And as the hot wet air rose from the sea into the storm the wind began to move in circles. An eye formed in the center of the circles of cloud and wind. At first the eye was wide, about 200 kilometers across, and the winds blew round and round the eye quite slowly. But as the storm traveled over the sea, the winds became stronger as more and more hot wet air rose up into the storm. The eye of the storm got smaller as the winds became stronger.

And all the time the storm continued to move west over the sea. It moved west, following the warm water that traveled west from the coast of Africa out into the Atlantic. The warm water moved thousands of miles across the Atlantic, towards the coast of North America. And like a wild dog chasing the smell of a kill, the storm followed the warm water. Day after stormy day, it traveled across the open ocean. And after a few days, on September 13, when the storm was less than 2000 kilometers from the Caribbean, the winds blew up to 120 kilometers an hour. Screaming, terrible, and dangerous, a hurricane was born.

The weather forecasters called the killer wind Hurricane Irene. And Hurricane Irene threw itself across the Atlantic, straight towards America. In front of it the hurricane pushed a huge wall of water, an eight meter high storm wave that would destroy anything in its way.

Chapter 2 *The hurricane gets closer*

September 16

The Wings School of Flying was not far from Miami. Max had been a student there for nearly a year. He had always wanted to fly, and he had always loved the wide open sky. As a small boy he loved watching the clouds during the day and looking at the stars at night. At Christmas other boys asked for toys, but all Max wanted were books about the stars and a telescope so he could look at them more closely. He spent night after night on the beach with his telescope, looking at the stars and learning their names. When other boys were playing tennis or going sailing, he stayed at home to study. He needed really good grades to get into flying school. And in the end his hard work was worth it. He was top of the class at high school, and the flying school accepted him immediately. And after all those years watching the sky, Max was able to fly right up into it. It was like a ride into another world, a new and empty world that was clean and beautiful, like a world that had only just begun.

But right now Max felt terrible and even the thought of his next flying lesson didn't help. It was lunchtime and he was sitting in the school cafetetia, looking unhappily out of the window at another beautiful sunny day. He could not stop thinking about Ikemi. He could not understand her. He had thought that she really liked him, he had thought that maybe she even loved him. And now, suddenly, she didn't want to see him again. Her father was more important to her than he was and that hurt him badly. He decided, unhappily, that the best thing to do was to forget her and get on with his life. But how could he get on with his life? Each minute of the day he thought about her, and each time he thought about her it hurt him.

One of Max's flying teachers, Ross Peters, sat down next to him. Max was one of Ross's favorite students. He was intelligent, serious, hardworking, and very quick to learn. Everyone liked Max. If anyone needed help or advice, they asked Max. Ross Peters looked at Max's unhappy face and smiled at him.

"What's the matter Max? Not hungry?" he asked.

Max shook his head. "No, sir, no, I'm not."

The teacher looked closely at Max. "Is there anything I can do to help?"

Max shook his head again. "No, it's OK, thanks. I'm OK."

Ross Peters began to eat his lunch. He had never seen Max look so unhappy before. "Did you hear about the hurricane out in the Atlantic, Max? They say it's a big one."

Max nodded. "Yeah. I heard something about it on the radio."

"I used to fly a hurricane hunter," Ross said.

Max looked at his teacher in surprise. "You flew a hurricane hunter! A plane that chases hurricanes? Wow! What's it like, flying into a hurricane?"

Ross Peters thought for a moment. "Well," he said slowly, "it's a lot more fun and a lot more frightening than the biggest Disney ride you've ever been on. There you are, flying along, and you know you're going to meet a wall of wind coming towards you at anything up to 200 kilometers an hour. And as well as the winds coming straight at you, there are all the winds inside the hurricane which are going up and down, up and down like elevators in an apartment building." He smiled. "But once you get inside the eye of the hurricane, it's amazing. There's no wind, the sky is a beautiful blue, and the sun shines. It's hard to believe there are killer winds all around you."

Ross looked at his watch and got up to go.

"By the way," he said, "Are you busy after school? I'll be working on my seaplane the *Manatee* again, and I could really use some help. I've started painting her now and I'm hoping to get her finished by the end of the week."

Max looked happier. "Yes, sir, I'd love to help. I'll come down and see you there after school."

Just then the music on the radio stopped. The room went quiet as students and teachers stopped talking to listen to the weather forecast.

"And now for a hurricane warning. Hurricane Irene, with winds up to 260 kilometers an hour, is traveling towards Cuba. Antigua, Nevis, Puerto Rico, the Dominican Republic, Cuba, and the coastal areas of southern Florida are under hurricane watch . . ."

The forecast ended and everyone began to talk at once.

"A hurricane! Wow! Do you think it will hit us? Do we need to leave the area?" asked one student.

"I don't think so," Ross Peters replied. "We get up to thirty hurricane warnings every year and nothing usually happens. Hurricanes often change course. It's very hard to tell which way they'll go. I don't think this hurricane will reach us."

*   *   *

In a small apartment in Key Biscayne, Ikemi was also listening to the hurricane warning. She turned off the radio and looked thoughtful. Her father had gone fishing yesterday evening. As usual, he went alone. As usual, he had only taken a cooler full of beer and a couple of loaves of bread. Ikemi sometimes tried to give him fruit, or cheese, or cookies to take onto the boat. But he never wanted it.

Hiru was a good fisherman. He always came home after a night or two with the cooler empty of beer but full of tasty fresh fish.

"Ikemi! How about sushi for lunch?" he always shouted as he came into the apartment. Ikemi always ran out to meet him and look at the fish he'd caught. Then he left his fishing things in the hall and carried the cooler into the kitchen. He tied a scarf around his head like a sushi chef in a Japanese restaurant, and together they cooked the rice and cut up the fish. Sushi was Ikemi's favorite meal.

Ikemi decided it was too soon to start worrying about her father. She went over to the window and looked out. It was another beautiful calm day. "I'm sure he'll come back by this evening," she said to herself. "He'll hear the hurricane warning and he'll come straight back. He won't stay out all night with a hurricane coming." She packed her books and checked the time. She should go to school, she had a class in an hour. There was nothing she could do.

"He'll be back soon," she said. She picked up her things and left the apartment. Soon she was driving into Miami and parking in the school parking lot. She hurried. She didn't want to be late for her class.

*   *   *

At the same time, a long way out to sea, Hiru was having a good day. It was wonderful weather for fishing. The sea was calm, and the sky was cloudless. He had caught lots of fish already. He opened a beer and continued to watch his line as it disappeared into the water. Maybe today he'd catch a really big fish. He certainly felt lucky. He took a long drink of the cold beer. Life was good.

Since the death of his wife, Hiru had spent most of his free time on the sea, fishing. He had bought the boat a year after she died. She had died slowly, little by little. It was a bad death and the pain of it had almost destroyed him. He was left alone with Ikemi. For a long time Ikemi was the only person he could talk to. He turned his back on family and friends who tried to help him. He did not answer the door or the telephone. He only wanted to be left alone. He did not want sad-faced people sitting in his house telling him how sorry they were. He did not want kind neighbors bringing nicely cooked food for him and the child. He did not want friends to put their arms around his shoulders and tell him that the pain would get better in time. He did not want the pain to get better. The pain was important to him. The pain and the anger he felt kept her near to him, kept her alive. But he could not explain that to all those kind and noisy people who wanted him to forget his pain, forget his anger, make new friends, meet new people, forget her. So he bought a boat. A strong little fishing boat. He called the boat the *Elizabeth*, his wife's name. And when he could, he left Ikemi with friends or family and went out to sea on the *Elizabeth*.

At first the sea was just an escape from the awful emptiness his wife's death had left behind. On the *Elizabeth*, he could be alone with his pain, alone with his anger, alone with his sadness. It was only here, far from all those too friendly, too loud Americans that he could find peace. And little by little the pain and the anger left him. The stillness of the sea on calm days made him feel better, the waves on stormy days made him wildly happy, and the bite of a fish on the end of his line made him forget his pain. And so it was that the sea saved him.

But now, years later, he needed the sea as much as ever. He needed to fish. He respected the fish he caught. He respected them because they were brave, they were clever, they were strong, and they fought hard. They fought hard, they fought long, and they never stopped fighting until they were out of the water and no hope was left. Hiru respected the fish he caught a lot more than he respected the Americans he did business with. He did not really understand Americans.

Hiru often wished he had gone back to Japan after Elizabeth had died. But by then Ikemi was already doing well at her American school. She had friends, a beautiful place to grow up in and she spoke English much better than Japanese. Hiru had taken her to Tokyo a few times, but she didn't like the crowded narrow streets, the noise, the food, the long, boring evenings with her Japanese cousins. She always wanted to get back to Florida, to her friends, to the sea, to the free life she enjoyed in America. Hiru began to think that his beautiful daughter was like a fish, swimming free in the ocean. He did not want to catch her and shut her in the narrow streets of Tokyo and small rooms of a Tokyo apartment. She was not a thing to catch and put in a small glass bowl. He did not want to fight her. She needed to be free. So Hiru had decided to stay in Florida.

He opened another beer and looked at his watch. It was almost time for the weather forecast. He got up to turn on the radio. Then there was a pull on his line. Another fish! He sat down quickly and began to pull the line in. There was another pull on the line, then another. It was a big fish! Quickly, he let out some line. The fish was fighting hard. Hiru stood up and looked over the side of the boat. This fish was bigger than anything he'd caught so far – and he'd been fishing in these waters for years. Hiru got ready for a fight. Little by little, he pulled the line in when he felt the fish was resting. When the fish decided to run, he let the line out. The fish was fighting bravely. Hiru fought back, slowly pulling the big fish in. He fought the fish for five, ten, fifteen minutes. The fish fought back. Slowly, he pulled the fish nearer. It was going to be a long fight and Hiru forgot about the weather forecast on the radio. This was it, this was the big one!

Chapter 3 *The hurricane kills*

September 17

The beautiful Caribbean island of Antigua was the first island to be hit by Hurricane Irene. The islanders had heard the hurricane warnings. They had lifted their boats out of the water and tied them to the ground. They had put shutters, heavy pieces of wood, in front of their windows to stop the storm from breaking the glass. The islanders had bought so much food and water that the stores were soon empty. They knew that the hurricane might destroy the island's gas stations and that after the hurricane had passed there might be no fresh water for days. They had put gas in their cars and water in their bathtubs.

Most people living close to the sea packed their valuables, their children, dogs and cats into their cars. They closed and locked their homes and went to stay with friends or family in safer parts of the island. Vacationers in coastal areas were not happy when their hotels were closed, but they had no choice. They were taken to stay in hotels higher up on the island where the storm waves could not reach them.

A group of twenty Americans on a week's sailing vacation in the island also knew about the hurricane. They brought their boat, the 40-meter *Wave Dancer*, into Nelson's Dock and tied it up to the jetty. They went into the town to find a hotel, but all the hotels were closed because of the hurricane. There was nowhere for them to go, so they returned to the boat for the night. *Wave Dancer* was large and heavy, and they thought they would be safe. After all, they were tied up to the jetty in shallow water only a few meters from land. Hurricane Irene hit them while they slept with 250 kilometers an hour winds. The eight-meter storm wave broke the strong lines holding the boat to the jetty. It lifted the boat up like a toy and turned it over like a piece of paper. Then it dropped the boat. The boat broke up like an egg dropped on a hard floor. All twenty people on the boat died.

*   *   *

Ikemi had not slept much during the night. Her father had still not returned. She put on a sweater and looked out of the window. She could feel a change in the weather. The sky was cloudy and gray, and the leaves of the palm trees were moving just a little in the light wind. The air felt different. It was colder. She checked the time and turned on the radio.

"Hurricane Irene hit the island of Antigua during the night and more than forty people have died. Many coastal towns were destroyed and thousands of people are homeless. Heavy rains from Irene are continuing to fall and winds have reached 274 kilometers an hour. If Irene does not change course, the hurricane will pass over the Dominican Republic and the island of Cuba within the next twenty-four hours and the coast of Florida in about forty-eight hours. People should leave coastal areas until the storm has passed."

Suddenly, Ikemi felt very worried. Where was her father? Why hadn't he come back? She tried to call him on his cellphone but he didn't answer.

"Maybe he's working on the boat at the marina. He just forgot to call me to tell me he's back."

She left the apartment and went down in the elevator and out into the parking lot. She got into her car and drove a few kilometers down the main street of Key Biscayne before taking a side road. The side road led through some palm trees before reaching a marina full of boats. The marina was busy and some people were taking their boats out of the water.

"Please be here!" thought Ikemi as she hurried to the place where her father kept his boat. But the boat was not there. Ikemi's father was still somewhere out at sea.

"I'm sure he'll hear the hurricane warnings on the radio," she said to herself as she drove slowly back to the apartment. But she was not really sure that he would. She knew that he did not always turn the radio on when he was fishing.

"I need peace and quiet to catch fish," he always said.

*   *   *

Hiru was not getting much peace and quiet in the boat. He had seen the weather changing early in the day. The beautiful blue sky began to cloud over and the wind began to get stronger. It was no longer warm. Maybe it was time to go home, before the wind got any stronger. But this was the best fishing ever! The cooler was full, and he was catching more and more. The fishing was so good he could not stop. It might never be this good again. He wasn't worried about the wind getting stronger or the sky getting darker. He had been out in strong winds and bad seas before, and he knew that the *Elizabeth* would get him home. So he threw on a sweater, and fished happily, knowing that he was not too far from the coast and could easily get back in an hour or two.

During the afternoon, the wind became much stronger and the fishing was not as good. But still he didn't stop. At last the sea became so rough and the sky looked so dark he decided it was time to go back. He put his fishing things away and tied the cooler down. It was difficult to stand up now, the boat was moving so much. He went across the boat, holding onto the sides of the boat to stop himself from falling. He turned the key to start the engine. The engine started, coughed, and died. Hiru turned the key again. Once more the engine started up and died. The third time Hiru tried, the engine did not start; or the fourth time, or the time after that.

Hiru checked the engine for problems. After an hour checking everything he could think of, Hiru still did not understand why the engine would not start. There was only one thing to do. He had to take the engine to pieces and clean it. This would take time. Ikemi would be worried if he was away for another night. He tried to call her on his cellphone, but he had no signal. He went down to the cabin and put on another sweater and a jacket. He made himself some coffee and then began working on the engine. He worked slowly and carefully. It was going to be a very long night.

*   *   *

On the island of Nevis, less than 2000 kilometers south-east of Miami, Elaine Bridges felt safe in her beautiful new seventh-floor apartment on Fig Tree Hill. The apartment building was very strong, and it was built well above the coast and the village where Elaine had lived as a child. She stood by the window and looked towards the village. She had been happy to leave it. The streets were narrow and dirty and the houses were small and uncomfortable. Her parents' house was crowded and dark.

She had left school when she was fourteen and started work. Her family needed money. There was not much work on the island and not much money for families in the crowded villages. Elaine had begun to work in the fish packing factory. It wasn't bad work. She could talk and joke to the other women who worked with her. But she hated the cold wet fish. After only half an hour her hands became red and as cold as the large pieces of ice the fish were packed in. And she hated the smell of fish everywhere – on her hands, her face, her clothes, her hair. The first thing she did when she got home in the evening was throw her clothes into the sink and take a shower. She stood under the thin stream of water and washed her hair again and again. But it seemed to her that the smell of fish never left her.

Sometimes she dreamed about having a husband and family and her own home to look after. Elaine sometimes looked at the older women working beside her, women in their forties and fifties. They joked and laughed like the young girls, but their faces were tired, their hair had gray in it, and their bodies were shapeless. Elaine hoped that she would not still be working in the factory when she was forty. She hoped she would meet a rich and handsome man who would take her away from the factory and put her into a beautiful apartment. But it was difficult to find men like that. Then she met Rick.

Rick was a schoolteacher, twelve years older than she was and not very handsome. But his face was kind and he had a good job as Principal of the nearby school. She had agreed to marry him and now her dream had come true – here she was living in this lovely new apartment with two beautiful baby girls born just six days ago. She smiled. She turned away from the window and put on some water to make tea. She made two cups, added lots of milk and sugar, and carried one cup into the living room.

Rick was outside on the narrow balcony of the apartment where they used to sit in good weather. He was putting the storm shutters over the windows. It was a difficult job in the narrow balcony in the strong wind, and he dropped one of the shutters with a crash.

"Shh! Quiet, honey!" she shouted through the balcony door. "Don't make so much noise! You'll wake the babies!"

Rick picked up the shutter and shouted back.

"If those babies can sleep through the noise of this wind, they can sleep through anything! What do you want me to do? Wait until they wake up?"

Elaine looked out over the island. It was raining so hard she couldn't even see the sea. But she thought she could hear the wild crashing of the waves above the noise of the wind.

"Well, no, honey . . ."

"The hurricane might hit any time! You want me to wait for the babies to wake! We should have left the island two days ago for somewhere safer. But no. You said the babies were too young to travel. You said it would be too difficult to move them. You said you didn't feel well enough to leave the apartment. You said we'd be fine with the storm shutters up. Then everybody else goes to stay someplace safe, and here we are with one of the worst hurricanes in years coming straight for us. And you say I'm making too much noise?"

Elaine took the tea back to the kitchen and then went into the babies' room to see if they were awake. She was happy to see they were still asleep. Elaine couldn't understand how they could sleep through the noise of the wind and the rain. Such lovely babies! Only six days' old and so beautiful. Little hands, little faces, little heads of soft black hair. She looked round the room. It was painted yellow, with yellow and white curtains. There were pictures on the walls, and pretty painted furniture stood around the room. The little beds were painted different colors, and there were two little cupboards for the babies' clothes. Well, her babies were going to be the best-dressed, best-loved, cleverest babies in the Caribbean!

She walked over to the window. It was getting windier, and some of the palm trees looked like they were almost touching the ground. Yes, the wind was much stronger now than a few minutes ago. She put her hand on the window and could feel the glass moving backwards and forwards in the wind. She couldn't believe it. How could the glass move in and out like that without breaking?

"Rick!" she shouted. "Rick! Come here! Put up the shutters here!" But just then the hurricane hit the building which shook it as if it had been hit by a train.

"Rick!" There was no reply, only the horrible screaming

noise of the wind and horrible, loud noises coming from the building itself.

She ran over to the balcony door, but she could not see Rick. "Dear God, the wind has blown him off the balcony!" she thought. The rain was falling so heavily and the sky was so dark that it could almost have been night. Then at the far end of the balcony, she saw something move. It was Rick. He was on his knees, with his arms around the metal rails of the balcony. His head was down and the heavy storm shutters had blown out of his hands.

"Rick!" she screamed again. Rick began to pull himself along the balcony, head still down, holding onto the rails. Halfway along the balcony, he stopped. She could see he was tired. The wind was blowing harder than ever. A huge piece of metal, probably the roof of a house, came flying up into the air. It flew straight at the balcony, and crashed against the rails. Then the piece of metal fell, taking with it some of the rails and the wall of the apartment below them. There was nothing to stop the wind blowing Rick off the balcony. He had stopped moving. She wondered if the metal had hit him.

"Rick! Come on! Come on!" she screamed. She was crying when he began to move again. Slowly, he pulled himself along the balcony, head down. After what seemed like hours, he reached the door. Elaine opened it, and he half fell, half pulled himself into the room. The wind blew into the room with him. Magazines and papers flew through the air, cups fell off the tables, chairs fell over.

"Help me shut the door!"

They both pulled the door shut.

"Rick! Are you all right? I was so afraid! I thought the wind had blown you away!"

Rick was shaking.

"I'm fine. Listen, Elaine! We have to move fast, the windows are going to break! Quick! Get the babies! Get into the bathroom!"

Elaine picked up the babies and they ran into the bathroom. It was a small room with no windows. Rick shut the door and locked it.

"Dear God, dear God, please look after us," whispered Elaine as she sat on the floor with the babies in her arms. The noise was terrible. And it was getting worse. Screaming like a wild animal, the wind threw itself at the building, shaking it like a dog shakes a rabbit. Then came a loud crash as the window of the babies' room broke, and another soon after as the living room window followed. The wind screamed into the apartment and they could hear the furniture crashing against the apartment walls. They heard the television crash to the floor and the sound of breaking glass as the hurricane destroyed the kitchen. The wind blew under the bathroom door and the shaking got worse. It was like a wild animal in the apartment was trying to kill them. Then suddenly, the lights went out and they were in darkness. Elaine screamed and the babies began to scream too, both at the same time.

"Rick! It's going to get us! We're all going to die! We're going to die!"

Chapter 4 *In the marina*

18 September

In the apartment, Ikemi turned the radio off slowly and sat down. There had been another hurricane warning. The hurricane was only twenty-four hours away now, and still her father had not returned. She felt sick and terribly afraid. This hurricane was a killer. Winds of 274 kilometers an hour would destroy anyone and anything. And the eight-meter storm wave that the hurricane was driving in front of it . . . what would happen to her father's little fishing boat if it was hit by an eight-meter wave? What would happen to her father?

The sky was getting darker now and the wind was getting stronger. Why hadn't he returned? What had happened? He was alone in his boat, somewhere out at sea, and a hurricane was coming. Maybe he was hurt, maybe the engine had broken down, maybe he was in some other kind of trouble: maybe, maybe, maybe . . .

She got up, threw on some clothes, and drove to the marina. The roads were very busy. People were leaving the island, planning to stay away from the coast until the hurricane had passed. In the marina all of the boats were out of the water, and most were tied down safely. One of the men who worked in the marina was tying down the last boat. He saw Ikemi and stopped for a moment.

"Hi, honey, what are you doing here? You should be going somewhere safe. There's a hurricane coming!"

"Yes, I know! But I think my father's still out at sea! He went fishing three days ago, and I haven't heard from him! He hasn't come back. Please, we've got to send somebody to look for him! He's in trouble, I know he is!"

The man shook his head.

"You aren't going to find anybody to go out with a hurricane coming," he replied. "You haven't got a chance. Everybody has their boats out of the water by now. You just get going, now." He turned back to his work.

"But I've got to find him!" Ikemi took hold of the man's arm. "I can't go and leave him out there! Please, we have to go and look for him!"

The man began to sound impatient.

"Listen, honey, I'm losing time. Your dad's got a radio on the boat. There have been hurricane warnings every hour. He must have gone someplace else, like Boca Raton. He sometimes fishes up there, doesn't he? So he just went to the nearest safe place. He'll be fine, you'll see."

"The radio! Can I use the radio in the marina office?" she asked the man. "Can I try to radio him on that?"

"If you want," he answered. "But you'd better hurry up. When I've got this boat tied down I'm going to lock up and get out of town."

The man turned his back to her and went on with his work.

Ikemi ran across the parking lot and into the office. She picked up the radio and spoke into it.

"*Elizabeth, Elizabeth, Elizabeth*, this is Biscayne Marina, Biscayne Marina. Over." There was no reply. She tried again.

"*Elizabeth, Elizabeth, Elizabeth*, this is Biscayne Marina,

Biscayne Marina. Over." Still there was no reply. The horrible silence over the radio made her feel worse than before. What had happened? Why hadn't he come back to land?

She put the radio down and went slowly back to her car. The wind was getting stronger and the waves were getting bigger. The sky was getting darker. She got into her car with a feeling of terrible, sick hopelessness. Just at that moment, her cellphone rang. She picked it up quickly.

"Hello, Daddy? Daddy? Is that you?" There was silence for a moment, then she heard Max's voice.

"No, it's me, Ikemi, it's Max. Are you OK?"

"No . . . no, no, I'm not! I'm not!"

"What's the matter? What's happened?" Max asked.

"It's Daddy . . . he went out fishing three days ago . . . he hasn't come back . . . I can't get anyone to help him . . . the hurricane will be here soon . . . oh Max, I'm so worried, I feel sick, and I don't know what to do!"

"Where are you? Ikemi! Tell me! Where are you?"

"In the marina . . ."

"Wait for me there! Don't go anywhere! I'll be there in ten minutes. Don't worry, we'll find him," Max said.

Ikemi put her phone away in her bag, put her head in her hands, closed her eyes, and cried. A few minutes later she heard the sound of a motorcycle stopping beside the car. She looked up and saw Max. She ran to him and threw her arms around him.

"Max! Oh, Max! Thank you for coming! I'm so happy to see you!"

Max looked at his watch.

"I came in seven minutes! Not bad! It's a good thing I've

got the motorcycle – the roads are impossible. Everyone is leaving the island." He took hold of her hand. "Come on. Jump on. Let's go."

"But where are we going?" Ikemi asked.

"We're going to find your father," Max replied.

Ikemi did not ask how he was going to find Hiru. She just knew that somehow, he would. She got onto the back of the motorcycle.

"Hold on!" he shouted.

She put her arms round him and rested her head against his back. She felt more hopeful now. They drove out onto the main road off the island. The road was crowded with cars, buses, trucks and vans. Everybody wanted to leave the island as quickly as possible, but there were so many cars on the road that the traffic had stopped completely. People were getting out of their cars and looking worriedly at the traffic ahead of them. A few people were shouting angrily, and dogs shut in cars were barking. A police helicopter was flying above, but there were no policemen on the road helping the traffic. Max drove slowly past the line of cars. It took them a long time to reach the flying school. There was nobody there. Max stopped the motorcycle in front of the building.

"Wait here!" he shouted. He disappeared into the building and came out a few minutes later with some keys.

"Off we go!" He got back onto the motorcycle, and they went down a narrow road behind the school building.

"Where are we going?" shouted Ikemi.

"You'll see!" he replied.

Ten minutes later the road ended at a narrow beach. There was an old wooden jetty at the end of the beach, and beyond that, on the open water, was the oldest, dirtiest, ugliest seaplane Ikemi had ever seen.

Max stopped the bike. "Ikemi, let me introduce you to the *Manatee*! Isn't it beautiful?"

Ikemi looked at the plane.

"Max, are you sure that plane can fly?"

"Of course it can fly! I know it looks old. It's an old plane, but it's strong and heavy. It belongs to one of my teachers. He bought her a few months ago. It needed a bit of paint and a bit of mending, and I've been helping him."

"But . . . do you know how to fly it?"

Max took Ikemi's hand and led her along the jetty. At the end of the jetty he stopped and smiled at her.

"Don't worry, Ikemi. We'll be OK. It may be an interesting flight, but if your father is still out there, we'll find him. And then we'll bring him back."

*　　*　　*

Hiru was still at sea. He had worked on the engine for most of the night and when the first light in the stormy sky showed it was morning, he was ready to start the engine. If it did not start now, it never would. He looked quickly at the sky and tried to start the engine. The engine turned once, twice, then died. He tried again. Once more the engine came to life, turned a few times, then died. For a third time he tried.

"Come on, come on, come on!"

The engine coughed, and died. Just like yesterday. Hiru tried again and again, but he knew the engine was not going to start. Suddenly, a large wave broke over the boat and water came in. Hiru began to pump out the water. There was a lot of water, and he was tired. He had not slept that night and had not eaten since the day before. He knew he needed help. He knew that the *Elizabeth* might not be able to get him home this time. He pumped out the water and then turned on the radio. He picked up the radio and, holding himself against the side of the boat, spoke clearly and loudly against the screaming of the wind and the crashing of the waves.

"Mayday, Mayday, Mayday! This is the fishing boat *Elizabeth*, fishing boat *Elizabeth* . . ." He said where his boat was. "My engine is not working and I am in danger of sinking. I need help immediately." He listened. There was no friendly voice, answering from a boat nearby. He repeated his message, then listened again. Still there was no reply. How come there were no other boats around? There must be other fishing boats in the area, or big ships on their way into Miami. He was about to speak for the third time when he heard a voice on the radio. He turned it up and listened carefully.

"Hurricane alert, hurricane alert, all coastal areas of Florida. Hurricane Irene is passing over the island of Cuba and is expected to hit the coast of Florida in less than twenty-four hours. There may be winds of up to 274 kilometers an hour and a storm wave of eight meters or more. Everyone should leave coastal areas as soon as possible."

Hiru quietly put the radio down. Now he understood why nobody was answering his Mayday calls. There weren't any other boats around. They all knew that a hurricane was coming.

Hiru was wet, he was cold, he was tired, and he was afraid. The sky was dark and angry and the wind was blowing hard. The waves were throwing the boat around like children throwing a ball. The storm was getting worse, the wind was getting stronger, and the waves were getting even bigger as the minutes passed.

The waves were the biggest Hiru had ever seen. They were like great moving mountains of water. His eyes were red and hurt from the salt water which blew into them when he looked up. He felt sick because the waves were so big that the *Elizabeth* was going up and down like some wild carnival ride. They lifted the boat up as they passed under it and then dropped it like a stone. The little boat shook as it crashed down from the waves and then lay at the bottom of the wave. This was the most dangerous moment because if a wave broke over the boat, water came in. Hiru pumped the water out of the boat. But every time he did another wave broke over the boat, and Hiru had to pump the water out again. Pumping the water out was hard work, and as the waves got bigger it was taking longer and longer to pump the boat dry.

Hiru began to feel sick and very tired. The engine was dead; there was no hope of returning to Miami. He could not reach anyone by radio or phone; there was no hope of someone coming to help him. But he had to try and stay alive. That meant pumping the boat until the hurricane was over. How long did hurricanes last? Two days? Three?

"How long can I last?" Hiru wondered. He had not slept for twenty-four hours. He was hungry. He was very tired.

He was cold. His body hurt from the pumping. And above all he was angry that he was going to die stupidly and leave Ikemi to look after herself. What would Elizabeth think about that? Hiru began to pump fast. "My body is just a machine," he said to himself, "and I'm not going to let it stop working. I'm just going to keep on going till I get back home. Elizabeth, you've got to help me."

Chapter 5 *Good to be alive*

Hurricane Irene blew over Nevis and screamed away to Puerto Rico, the Dominican Republic, and Cuba. Before the hurricane, Nevis had been a green island, with lots of palm trees and fields of pineapples. After the hurricane, the island was brown. All the palm trees growing along the beaches, along the roads, and on the hills had been blown away by the wind. The marina was no longer there, and any boat left in the water had been smashed to pieces. All the houses in the coastal areas had been destroyed. A pineapple farmer, hurrying to check his fields, found that all his pineapples had been washed away by the storm wave. He also found a ten-meter boat lying in one of his fields. It was 500 meters from the sea.

On Fig Tree Hill, it was impossible to drive along the roads. There were palm trees in the roads, and cars and buses and big trucks were lying on their sides. There were roofs of buildings that had blown off, broken glass everywhere, and all kinds of things which had been blown out of people's houses – beds, tables, chairs – and everything wet and dirty.

Many houses did not have roofs, and the wind had blown the walls away from others. There was no electricity on the island, and there was no water. All the telephone lines were down. It was impossible for people to call for an ambulance, and anyway it was impossible for ambulances to use the roads. People climbed slowly over things in the road, hoping to find something useful to rebuild their homes. Some people searched buildings for lost family, shouting their names. Others went into stores and tried to take as much food and as many things as they could steal. People slowly began to count the dead.

In the apartment building at the top of the hill, Rick and Elaine were standing in the babies' room. They were tired, hungry, and dirty, but they were alive. The room they were standing in was empty. The wind had blown everything out of it. There was glass all over the floor, and the walls and carpet were wet and dirty. The babies' beds, their cupboards, the little chairs and the prettily painted table, the flowered curtains, and the colorful pictures were all gone. The living room was full of broken furniture, and in the kitchen every plate and cup had been broken. Rick and Elaine stood hand-in-hand looking at what was left of their beautiful home. The babies lay sleeping in a towel in the bathroom.

Elaine looked at Rick and kissed him hard on the nose. "Honey, I love you so much!"

He picked her up in his arms. Together they danced round the room. It was good to be alive.

*   *   *

That evening, all the American newspapers had a front page story about the hurricane:

CUBA HIT BY WORST STORM IN 50 YEARS

Hurricane Irene, one of the largest storms ever to hit the Caribbean, cut through Cuba early this morning. About 200,000 people have left their homes. Tourists also had to leave their hotels in Varadero beach before the worst winds arrived.

Irene is a category four hurricane with winds of up to 274 kilometers an hour. Weather forecasters are saying that Irene is now heading for the southern tip of Florida, which is under a hurricane warning. Forty-five thousand people have left the Florida Keys over the last two days and air ambulances have lifted a hundred patients from two hospitals.

Chapter 6 *The* Manatee

Max and Ikemi walked along the jetty. The wind was strong and it began to rain. A small wooden boat, just big enough for two people, was tied to the end of the jetty. Max helped Ikemi down the steps and into the boat. He started the engine.

"Untie us!" he shouted. Ikemi untied the rope and Max took the boat into the open water. He did not go fast. The wind was blowing against them, and waves broke over the little boat and water came in.

"Not far to go!" Max shouted "We'll be there in a minute!" He kept his eyes on the waves and tried to take the boat through them. Ikemi looked at the water in the bottom of the boat, looked at the waves which were getting bigger as they left the land behind, and then looked at the *Manatee*. The *Manatee* looked very far away. The boat was going very slowly and a lot of water was coming in. Ikemi began to throw the water out of the boat. A lot of the salty water blew back into her face and hurt her eyes, but she kept throwing it out. It came in faster than she could throw it out, and by the time it had reached the *Manatee*, the boat was almost half full of water. It was raining hard now, and they were both wet and cold.

"Quick! Get inside!" Max unlocked the door in the seaplane's side and helped Ikemi climb inside. He followed and quickly shut the door. Inside the plane it was much quieter. Ikemi looked round. The inside of the plane was empty. There were only three seats at the front and a big yellow bag just behind them.

"Why aren't there any seats here in the back?"

Max was already sitting down and putting on his seat belt.

"The plane was used as an air ambulance up and down the Keys."

Max pushed the wet hair out of his eyes and began to look through some maps. He pulled one out.

"Ikemi, come and look."

Ikemi went up and sat in the seat next to Max. He showed her the map.

"Look. This is where we are. This is Key Biscayne and this is the marina. Now, where do you think your father might be?"

Ikemi looked at the map. There was a lot of water on the map, and not much land. She put her finger down east of Key Biscayne, about fifteen kilometers out to sea.

"He often goes around here."

Her finger moved up the coast.

"But he sometimes goes up the coast, towards Boca Raton. He goes where the fish are . . ."

"And he didn't say where he was going?"

Ikemi shook her head. "No, he didn't."

The wind suddenly hit the plane and shook it.

"We'd better go," he said. "We haven't got much time. OK. We'll go east from here, for about 15 kilometers."

"Then we'll be going straight into the hurricane," said Ikemi. "Max, are you sure you can fly this thing? What happens if we fly into the hurricane?"

"Don't worry," said Max. "Ross Peters taught me to fly

the *Manatee*. I've been up with him quite a few times. And as for flying into the hurricane – if a small light plane like a hurricane hunter can fly in storm winds, then a heavy old plane like the *Manatee* will just sail through." Max sounded very sure of himself, and Ikemi felt better.

"And anyway, we've got a very nice life raft if anything goes wrong." He looked at the big yellow bag lying on the floor behind the seats. "If we have problems landing the plane, drop it into the sea and jump in. There's water in there. Chocolate, a light, a radio . . . everything you need for a nice few days at sea!"

Ikemi wished he hadn't told her about the life raft.

"We're flying towards a hurricane in an old, broken-down seaplane and you think a life raft is going to make me feel any better? Are you crazy?"

Max held her hand for a second. "Come on, put on your seat belt. Let's go."

He started the engine. "Are you ready?" He turned to Ikemi. "Are you going to be OK?" he said.

Ikemi nodded. "I'll be fine," she said, "and Max . . . thank you."

Max did not reply. He was taking the plane into open water for the takeoff. The heavy plane moved slowly because the wind and the waves were pushing it back.

"Come on, come on, come on," whispered Max.

Ikemi shut her eyes. Then suddenly they were in the air.

"We're off!" said Max.

Ikemi looked through the window at the sea below. The clouds were very low and dark and the rain was heavy. It was very hard to see anything out of the window.

"We'll have to stay below the clouds," shouted Max, "or we won't be able to see anything!"

Ikemi could not see very far. The sky was dark and the rain was falling heavily. The waves below were dark, too, only showing white when they broke. "This is impossible," she thought to herself. "How can we find a little boat in this weather when we don't even know where it is?"

It was as though Max could read her thoughts.

"Don't worry. We'll find him," he said. And she believed him.

*　　*　　*

And as the *Manatee* began its journey east over the sea, Hurricane Irene was moving west. The hurricane left the broken island of Cuba behind and began to move over the water towards Miami. It brought with it great walls of cloud, heavy rain, and high winds. The great walls of cloud formed circles around the hurricane's eye.

The eye was at the center of the hurricane. It was a place of calm and peace. As the storm passed, first came the screaming winds and the biting rains which destroyed everything they blew over. Then, as the eye passed over, the winds and the rain stopped. No wind blew inside the eye, there was bright sunshine and a warm blue sky. You might think that the hurricane had passed – until the wall of the hurricane hit from the other side. Sometimes the eye is as little as six kilometers wide, sometimes as big as 60 kilometers wide. The smaller the eye, the faster the winds blow round it. Irene's eye was only 15 kilometers wide, and the winds around the eye were screaming, killing winds of

274 kilometers an hour, blowing up waves over eight meters high.

Hurricane Irene moved slowly over islands, beaches, villages, towns, and the open sea. Nothing could stop it. Like a careless child, the hurricane picked up anything that lay in front of it, then threw it down. Houses, ships, trucks, roofs, trees, people, animals were all lifted up, then thrown down as Irene passed by.

Chapter 7   *The last call*

Hiru stopped pumping the water out of the boat. There was too much water coming in. He was too tired and too cold. He had been pumping for several hours now, but every few minutes another wave broke over the boat. He could not pump fast enough. For the last few hours, he had stopped pumping every ten minutes to make a Mayday call on the radio. He heard the hurricane warnings, and he knew that the hurricane was only a couple of hours away. He knew the end was coming. The *Elizabeth* was strong, but not strong enough to go through a hurricane. The boat would break up when the hurricane hit it.

Hiru knew this, but he did not really care. He was so tired that all he wanted to do was to lie down and sleep. He could not fight the wind and the waves anymore. He left the pump and went to the cabin door. Slowly he went down the steps and closed the door behind him. There was a lot of water in the cabin, too, but at least the tops of the beds were out of the water. It would be wonderful to lie down on one of the beds, pull a blanket around his cold wet body, and go to sleep. He pulled a blanket from a small cupboard and put it around him. Before he lay down, he decided to make one last Mayday call. Shaking with the cold, sick and dead tired, he picked up the radio.

"Mayday, Mayday, Mayday, this is the *Elizabeth, Elizabeth, Elizabeth*. I am sinking. I need immediate help.

Over." He listened. Nothing. He reached over to put the radio back.

"*Elizabeth, Elizabeth, Elizabeth*, this is the *Manatee, Manatee.* Where are you? Where are you? Over."

At first, Hiru could only look at the radio as if it had bitten him. Was he dreaming? Then he heard the voice again.

"*Elizabeth, Manatee.* Where are you? Where are you? Over!"

No, the voice was real. There was another boat out there! They would help him! Hiru took the radio and almost shouted:

"*Manatee*, this is *Elizabeth*. I am about 10 kilometers east of Key Biscayne. Over"

"*Elizabeth, Manatee.* We'll be with you in about five minutes. Can you light flares to help us to see you? Over."

"*Manatee, Elizabeth.* I have flares. I will light them every three minutes, starting in three minutes. Out."

Hiru threw off the blanket. He did not feel tired any more, or hungry, or cold. He found a box of flares in a small cupboard near the door of the cabin. Then he climbed up the stairs two at a time, opened the cabin door, and fell out onto the deck of the boat. The water came well over his knees and the boat was sitting dangerously low in the water. He shut the cabin door, looked at his watch, and reached for the pump. By now the pump was underwater, but it didn't take long to find. He began to pump fast. Slowly, the water got lower. After two minutes, he stopped pumping and picked up the box of flares. He took one out and fired it up at the dark sky. A bright white light flew up into the sky over the boat. Suddenly, the dark sky turned bright. Hiru began to pump again, hard and fast. Another huge wave broke over the boat.

"He's still alive! He's still alive!" whispered Ikemi when she heard Hiru's voice over the radio. "Hurry up, Max! Hurry up!"

Max did not say anything. It was very difficult to fly the plane so close to the water, and the wind was so strong it was hard to keep it straight. And now that he knew that Hiru was waiting for them, he wondered just how he was going to land on those terrible, huge waves below them. And even if they landed safely, how was he going to get close enough to the *Elizabeth* to get Hiru off the boat and onto the plane? And even if he did that, how was he going to take off again in the huge waves? It had been hard enough to take off in the much calmer water near the coast – now they were out at sea and the waves were huge. Max suddenly felt very cold. He realized that if he tried to land, the *Manatee* would break up. Both he and Ikemi would die, as well as Hiru. He felt sick. What could he say to Ikemi? "Well, Ikemi, I'm terribly sorry but I can't land here, it's too stormy, and I can't save your father, and I was mad to think that I could. But we can get a good look at the *Elizabeth* sinking from the air."

Suddenly, through the rain, he could see a bright white light.

"Look! There it is! There's the flare! Over there! He's over there!" shouted Ikemi.

He looked quickly at her. She was smiling and her face was alive with hope. She seemed to be quite sure he was going to save her father. Max looked back out into the rain.

How could he tell her that he had brought her here just to watch her father die?

On the *Elizabeth*, Hiru heard the sound of an engine. Thank God! It was the boat! Soon he would be safe! The boat was coming to save him! He took out another flare and fired it. Great clouds of bright red smoke lit the darkness. He waved the flare. The sound of the engine got nearer. He looked for the boat but could see nothing. Then, suddenly, out of the wind and the rain a seaplane appeared. A plane? The pilot must be mad! He couldn't land the plane in these waves. It was impossible. Completely impossible! What was the pilot trying to do? Kill himself? Hiru stopped waving the flare. The flare died and he threw it into the waves. His hope died, too. This was the end. He was going to die.

As he flew the *Manatee* towards the *Elizabeth*, Max could see Hiru quite clearly in the light of the flare. He could see that the *Elizabeth* was lying very low in the water. Large waves were breaking over the boat all the time and Max could see that soon the boat would sink. There was very little time. Just then, a sudden strong wind hit the plane. Ikemi screamed. It took a few moments before Max was able to straighten the plane. By that time, they were flying over the sinking boat. Max saw Hiru stop waving the flare and knew what that meant. Hiru had realized that the plane could not land and save him.

"Ikemi!" he shouted, "listen carefully and do as I say! It's too rough here to land the plane. We'll have to wait until we're inside the eye."

"But . . . the boat's going to sink any minute . . ."

"Yes, I know. But we can drop him the life raft.

Remember? It's just behind the seat. It's a good one, a new one. If he gets into it and closes it, he'll be OK. You can throw it down to him."

"But how . . ."

"The life raft is on a long line. If you drop it in the right place, the wind and the waves will blow it onto the boat and your father can get it."

Ikemi did not ask any more questions. She took off her seat belt and got up.

On the *Elizabeth*, Hiru watched the *Manatee* disappear into the storm. Then, suddenly, over the radio:

"*Elizabeth, Manatee*! Sir, can you hear me? Over!"

Hiru crossed the boat like a man in a dream and picked up the radio.

"Who the hell is this?"

"It's me, it's Max, sir. Listen, I can't pick you up here, so I'm going to pick you up in the eye of the storm. I'm going to fly low over the boat. I'm going to drop you a life raft. There's a long line on the life raft. The wind will blow the line onto the boat. Tie yourself into the raft and make sure you close the raft. We'll pick you up inside the eye."

Hiru stood in his sinking boat like a man who'd been hit on the head. Max? Not Max, Ikemi's loud American friend? Max who drove a motorcycle too fast, spoke too loudly, and was training to be a pilot at flying school. Hiru felt himself go even colder. Max had said, "We'll pick you up in the eye.". Who was "we"? Don't let Ikemi be on that awful old plane with that crazy American boy in this terrible storm, please no . . .

"Max, is Ikemi with you? Listen to me! Fly back right now. Right now, do you hear me? Don't worry about me,

I'll be all right, just take Ikemi back right now, right now, do you hear me?"

"Sorry, sir, we didn't come all this way for nothing. Light a flare. Get ready to catch hold of the life raft line in about two minutes. Out!"

Max looked at Ikemi. "Get the life raft now!" he shouted. Ikemi got up and moved round the seats. The plane was being thrown around by the wind so much, it was difficult to stay standing up. She held onto the back of the seat.

"You're going to have to open the door. Make sure you hold on and don't fall out. When I shout 'Open' you open the door, and when I shout 'Drop', you drop the life raft. OK?"

"OK," replied Ikemi. She was so afraid, her hands were shaking. She picked up the life raft and stood by the door.

"OK," said Max, "there's the flare! This is it! Here we go!" He turned the plane quickly, and Ikemi almost fell over.

"Open the door!" he shouted.

Ikemi opened the door. The noise of the wind and the rain was terrible. A huge wind blew into the plane and almost knocked her off her feet. The wind was so strong she was sure it would blow her out into the water below. Holding the life raft with one hand and the back of Max's seat with the other, she looked out into the darkness. The plane was flying so low that Ikemi could feel the sea water being thrown against her face and in her eyes.

"Get ready!" shouted Max. Just ahead, between two huge waves, lay the *Elizabeth*. Hiru had fired another white flare and it was easy to see him. He was standing at the side of the boat, in a good place to catch hold of the line from the life raft. The water was now almost to Hiru's waist and the boat was sinking fast.

"Drop! Drop! Drop!" shouted Max.

Ikemi lifted the heavy life raft out of the door and dropped it. She could see it hit the water, then disappear under a wave.

"Shut the door, quickly!"

Ikemi put her body against the door and pushed hard. As soon as the door shut, it was quieter inside the plane.

"Well done!" shouted Max. Ikemi did not reply. She felt sick and she was shaking so much she could hardly walk. She went back to her seat slowly, sat down, and did up her seat belt.

"Did he get the line?" she asked Max. "Did you see? Has he got it?"

Chapter 8   *The eye of the storm*

On the *Elizabeth* Hiru shook his head as he put the radio down. It must be a dream, a bad dream. Ikemi had got her American boyfriend to fly out into a hurricane to save him. The boy must be completely mad. To fly into a hurricane in an old seaplane. What a crazy idea! Then to calmly tell Hiru that he was going to save him as if Hiru were a three-year-old child. It was unbelievable! But the boy was brave. And he was a fighter. And if that boy was going to try to fight the storm, then Hiru was going to fight it, too. Hiru did not think they were going to win this fight, but he was not going to give up before Max did.

Hiru watched the *Manatee* fly closer. The plane was flying very low and Hiru could see how much it was being thrown around by the wind. One moment it was at a safe height above the waves, then the next minute so low the waves were almost breaking over it. Hiru shook his head again. That boy certainly was mad – mad and brave. A huge wave broke over the *Elizabeth*. The boat began to sink. If Hiru could get into the life raft he had a chance, a very small chance, of being alive tomorrow. He climbed onto the top of the boat which was still above the water. From there, he could see the plane clearly in the light of the flare. It was very close. Suddenly a door in the side of the plane opened. A moment later, the bright yellow life raft was thrown out. There was a long line behind it.

Hiru watched the life raft and the line behind it fall. It

fell very close to the boat. Just then, the *Elizabeth* turned on her side and sank. Hiru fell into the water which seemed almost warm after the coldness of the wind. Almost immediately, he felt the line touch his neck. He put the line twice round his waist, then pulled. Slowly, he pulled himself along the line to the life raft at the other end. He took hold of the raft and pulled hard on a line. Like a beautiful yellow flower, the life raft opened up.

It was a big life raft, and very strong. Hiru pulled himself out of the water and into the raft. He just had time to close the raft before a huge wave hit it. The raft turned over and over, but very little water came in and after a few moments, Hiru could feel the raft turn right side up. This was not going to be very comfortable, but the raft might just be strong enough to get him through the hurricane. And if Max could get into the eye and pick him up there . . . he shook his head. He could not believe that Max was flying that plane up there. He certainly knew how to fly. The raft drop had been just right. And if Max could fly as well as that, there was just a chance that he could pick up Hiru in the eye.

Hiru tied himself onto the raft and began to look around. He found a light, some water, chocolate, and blankets. He ate the chocolate and drank some water. Away from the wind and the waves, warmed up by the blankets, Hiru felt a little better. But this was not a fishing trip he was going to forget.

On the *Manatee*, Max and Ikemi flew back over the water. They could not see the *Elizabeth*, and they could not see the life raft. The flare still lit the sky, but the sea was empty.

"It's gone down. The boat's gone down," whispered Ikemi. "Max! It's gone down! We were too late."

"Wait. Just wait a bit. Look! Over there!"

Suddenly, on the dark water, they saw the yellow life raft open up.

"He made it! He made it to the raft!"

Just then a wind hit the plane and threw it to one side, like a child throwing a toy plane across a room. Ikemi screamed.

"Look at this!" shouted Max. "The wind has gone up to 250 kilometers an hour in the last 90 seconds! This is it! We've hit the hurricane!"

A strong up-wind threw the plane into the air. The height meter jumped from 200 meters to 1300 meters in seconds. It was as if the plane was in a huge elevator, going up fast. Then just as suddenly, the plane began to fall like a stone. 1000 meters. 800 meters. 600 meters. 400 meters. Ikemi watched the height meter fall. It fell so fast.

"Max! Can't you stop it? We're going to hit the sea!"

300 meters, 200 meters. At 100 meters, Ikemi shut her eyes and put her head in her hands. Max was trying to pull the old seaplane out of the drop, but she was very slow.

"Come on, come on," whispered Max.

The height meter stopped going down at 50 meters. At last, the plane stopped falling. Max brought it back up to 200 meters. And suddenly, like a new world, they were in the eye of the storm. Above them the sky was clear and blue, and the sun was bright on the blue water below them. The sea was still quite rough, but there were no breaking waves and no wind.

"Well done, Max. We made it," Ikemi was staring

through the window at the calm and beautiful late afternoon sunshine.

"We'll have to pick up Hiru fast," said Max. "The eye is probably only about 20 kilometres wide."

He turned the plane and flew back. They could see the dark clouds of the hurricane and flew towards them. There was blue sea, blue sky, but no bright yellow life raft.

"Where is he?" asked Ikemi. It was not raining and she could see very clearly for several kilometers.

"He must be still inside the hurricane wall," replied Max. "But the storm will blow over him soon. We'll see him any minute."

Ikemi looked worried.

"But maybe the wind and the waves are pushing him towards the land. Maybe he won't come into the eye."

Max had not thought of that. The raft was small and light. The wind was blowing towards the land. The waves were traveling towards the land. The storm wave could easily carry the raft to land. Then it would send the raft crashing onto the land. It would hit the beaches, the rocks, the houses, and be thrown along the roads beside the sea. Hiru would die inside the life raft.

"He should be out of the wall by now," Ikemi was saying. "Where is he?"

"There he is! Over there! Over there!" Max shouted as the raft appeared. He turned the plane and flew over the life raft. The top of the raft was open and the raft was full of water. But as the plane came near, they could see Hiru. He was lying in the bottom of the raft, in the water. He was not moving.

"Get ready to land!" shouted Max. He had wanted to fly

around the raft several times to decide how to land, but now there was no time for that. He flew round the raft once and then brought the plane in to land. The *Manatee* jumped a couple of waves, then hit the water. The plane stopped not far from the raft. The moment the plane had come to a stop, Max took off his seat belt and put on a life-jacket. He tied a line onto the life-jacket and gave the other end to Ikemi.

"I'll swim over to him. I'll tie him to the line and you can pull us in. We haven't got much time." Ikemi nodded. Her face was white.

He jumped into the water and swam to the raft. Hiru's face and hands were cold and blue. Max put his face against Hiru's mouth. He was not breathing. Max looked back at Ikemi. She was standing very still by the door of the *Manatee*.

"Is he OK?" she shouted.

Max did not reply. He pulled himself into the raft. He held Hiru's head back and began to blow air into his mouth. Hiru's lips were cold as stone. As Max blew air into Hiru's mouth, his chest rose and fell. Max put his face against Hiru's mouth again, but still there was no breathing. He looked quickly at his watch and continued the mouth-to-mouth. How long could he do this before the hurricane hit them from the other side? They had to be back in the plane and in the air before it came. How long did they have? How fast was the storm traveling? Was Hiru dead? If he stayed too long like this, then he and Ikemi would die, too.

Once again he stopped the mouth-to-mouth to see if Hiru was breathing. He looked quickly at Ikemi. Her eyes were shut and her hands were together. As far as Max knew, Ikemi never went to church and didn't believe in God. It didn't look to Max as if he had much choice. He could either bring Hiru back to life or die when the storm hit them again. What he could not do was bring Ikemi the cold dead body of her father. He began mouth-to-mouth again.

"Max! Listen! The storm's getting close! It's coming!"

Max could already hear it, the noise of the storm. A few minutes ago it was a soft whisper, but now the noise was loud and angry.

"We've still got some time!" Max shouted.

Then Hiru coughed. It was the best sound Max had ever heard in his life. Max turned Hiru onto his side. He coughed again and was sick.

Max untied the line that held Hiru to the raft and tied on the line that Ikemi held.

"Pull us in!" he shouted. Ikemi pulled. Max held Hiru's head above the water. They got back to the plane and Max climbed up. They both pulled Hiru into the plane. He was breathing easily now, and his face was not so blue. They lifted him into a seat and did up the seat belt. Ikemi threw her jacket over him and held his cold hands.

"Daddy! Are you all right? Daddy! Daddy!"

Hiru opened his eyes.

At first, he did not seem to see anything. Then he looked at Ikemi and smiled. Slowly, his eyes began to move around the plane. He looked out of the door at the blue sky and the wall of noisy black clouds that were now very close. He watched Max shut the door of the plane and move quickly into the seat beside him. Max looked at him and saw that his face was its normal color and his breathing was normal.

"Let's get you home, sir."

Hiru nodded and listened to the engine start. The plane began to move.

*   *   *

The next day, Hiru was sitting in the hospital reception waiting for Ikemi to pick him up. The doctor had wanted him to stay in hospital for one night just to be safe, and he was feeling much better now. His night in hospital had also given him some time to really think about things, and especially about Ikemi.

Hiru looked up and smiled as Ikemi and Max came through the doors.

"Daddy, how are you feeling?" asked Ikemi.

"Hungry," Hiru replied.

He turned his head to Max who was standing quietly beside Ikemi.

"Max?" Hiru said.

"Yes, sir?"

"You like sushi?"

"Yes, sir," replied Max.

"You hungry?"

"Yes, sir."

"So where's the nearest sushi bar?" he asked.

Cambridge English Readers

Look out for other titles in the series:

Level 3

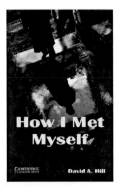

How I Met Myself
by David A. Hill

In a dark street in Budapest, John Taylor meets someone who changes his life. But who is this man? And what is he trying to tell John?

The House by the Sea
by Patricia Aspinall

Carl and Linda Anderson buy a holiday house by the sea. But one weekend Linda does not arrive at the house, and Carl begins to worry. What has happened to her?

A Puzzle for Logan
by Richard MacAndrew

Inspector Logan has a puzzle to solve: a murderer has escaped from a prison in Scotland and someone has found a young woman's body in a Holyrood Park. Are the events connected?

Double Cross
by Philip Prowse

Secret agent Monika Lundgren chases a would-be killer, and meets a mysterious football team, a rock musician, and a madman with dreams of world power . . .

The Ironing Man
by Colin Campbell

While Tom is at work in London, his wife Marina is left bored at home. She wishes for someone to do the housework for her and the Ironing Man enters her life. Soon everything begins to change for Marina and Tom.

The Beast *by Carolyn Walker*

'You may see something moving in the corner of your eye . . . I am following in the darkness behind you. I am your worst dream.'

On holiday in Wales, Susie meets the 'undead'. Is it a man or an animal?

The Lahti File
by Richard MacAndrew

'Foreign executive' Ian Munro is sent to Lahti in Finland to investigate some strange events. When the man he is there to meet is killed in front of him, Munro starts looking for answers and discovers a poisonous secret.

Two Lives *by Helen Naylor*

In the Small Welsh village of Tredonald, Megan and Huw fall in love. But is there love strong enough to last? Death, their families and the passing years are all against them.

Level 4

The Amsterdam Connection
by Sue Leather

Kate Jensen travels to Amsterdam to search for the murderer of a friend. She goes to parts of the city that tourists never see, meets a man prepared to kill to hide the truth, and discovers that football can be a very dangerous game.

But Was it Murder?
by Jania Barrell

Alex Forley had everything, but now he is dead. Detective Inspector Rod Eliot wants the answers to two simple questions. Was it murder? And if so, who did it?

The Lady in White
by Colin Campbell

While John, a successful TV producer, is researching a new programme, he comes across a story about a ghostly hitch-hiker which bears similarities to events in his own life.

Nothing but the Truth
by George Kershaw

Hu is a student in Bangkok, Thailand. She has a problem with a dishonest teacher, and is unsure what to do. Eventually she realises she must tell nothing but the truth.

60

When Summer Comes
by Helen Naylor

Stephen and Anna Martins take a holiday break in a seaside village to escape the stress of London. They meet and become friendly with a local fisherman. But when Stephen is called back to London, their lives start to change.

High Life, Low Life
by Alan Battersby

Private Investigator Nathan Marley is on his way to another day at the office. But a meeting with a homeless woman and a surprise letter change all that. Marley begins an investigation that takes him to the richest and poorest parts of New York city.

Staying Together
by Judith Wilson

Ikuko goes to England to study, promising to return to Japan to get married. But in Birmingham, Ikuko makes lots of new friends, including a man called Bernard. Ikuko must decide whether to keep her promise or follow her heart.

A Matter of Chance
by David A. Hill

Paul Morris's life in Italy changes when his wife dies suddenly. Then he meets Sandra and agrees to go on a trip with her. But Paul soon finds himself involved in a world of international crime and a car chase across Europe.